What can you see?

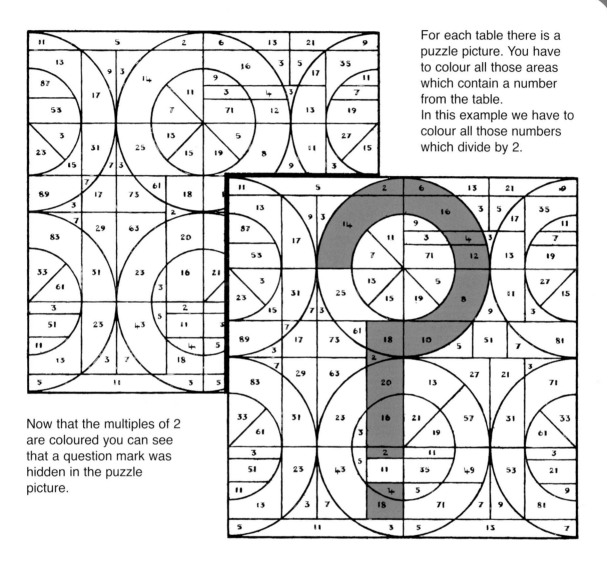

For each table there is a puzzle picture. You have to colour all those areas which contain a number from the table.
In this example we have to colour all those numbers which divide by 2.

Now that the multiples of 2 are coloured you can see that a question mark was hidden in the puzzle picture.

Multiples of any number create a particular pattern in the number square.
For each multiplication table, colour all the multiples to see what pattern it makes.

two

Two times table

1	X	2	=
2	X	2	=
3	X	2	=
4	X	2	=
5	X	2	=
6	X	2	=
7	X	2	=
8	X	2	=
9	X	2	=
10	X	2	=
11	X	2	=
12	X	2	=

Complete this table.

Multiples of two

1	2	3	4	5	6	7	8	9	10
11	12	13	14	15	16	17	18	19	20
21	22	23	24	25	26	27	28	29	30
31	32	33	34	35	36	37	38	39	40
41	42	43	44	45	46	47	48	49	50
51	52	53	54	55	56	57	58	59	60
61	62	63	64	65	66	67	68	69	70
71	72	73	74	75	76	77	78	79	80
81	82	83	84	85	86	87	88	89	90
91	92	93	94	95	96	97	98	99	100

Make a pattern by colouring all the numbers
which are multiples of 2.

Solve the puzzle picture opposite by colouring
just those numbers which divide by 2.
What can you see?

Picture Puzzle

three

Three times table

1	×	3	=
2	×	3	=
3	×	3	=
4	×	3	=
5	×	3	=
6	×	3	=
7	×	3	=
8	×	3	=
9	×	3	=
10	×	3	=
11	×	3	=
12	×	3	=

Complete this table.

Multiples of three

1	2	3	4	5	6	7	8	9	10
11	12	13	14	15	16	17	18	19	20
21	22	23	24	25	26	27	28	29	30
31	32	33	34	35	36	37	38	39	40
41	42	43	44	45	46	47	48	49	50
51	52	53	54	55	56	57	58	59	60
61	62	63	64	65	66	67	68	69	70
71	72	73	74	75	76	77	78	79	80
81	82	83	84	85	86	87	88	89	90
91	92	93	94	95	96	97	98	99	100

Make a pattern by colouring all the numbers
which are multiples of 3.

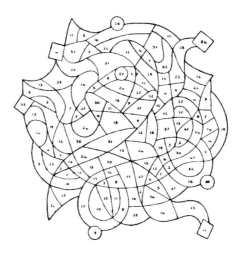

Solve the puzzle picture opposite by colouring
just those numbers which divide by 3.
What can you see?

Picture Puzzle

four

Four times table

1	X	4	=
2	X	4	=
3	X	4	=
4	X	4	=
5	X	4	=
6	X	4	=
7	X	4	=
8	X	4	=
9	X	4	=
10	X	4	=
11	X	4	=
12	X	4	=

Complete this table.

Multiples of four

1	2	3	4	5	6	7	8	9	10
11	12	13	14	15	16	17	18	19	20
21	22	23	24	25	26	27	28	29	30
31	32	33	34	35	36	37	38	39	40
41	42	43	44	45	46	47	48	49	50
51	52	53	54	55	56	57	58	59	60
61	62	63	64	65	66	67	68	69	70
71	72	73	74	75	76	77	78	79	80
81	82	83	84	85	86	87	88	89	90
91	92	93	94	95	96	97	98	99	100

Make a pattern by colouring all the numbers
which are multiples of 4.

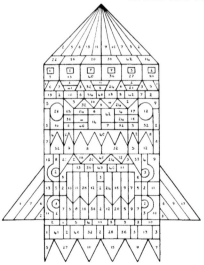

Solve the puzzle picture opposite by colouring
just those numbers which divide by 4.
What can you see?

Picture Puzzle

five

Five times table

1	X	5	=	
2	X	5	=	
3	X	5	=	
4	X	5	=	
5	X	5	=	
6	X	5	=	
7	X	5	=	
8	X	5	=	
9	X	5	=	
10	X	5	=	
11	X	5	=	
12	X	5	=	

Complete this table.

Multiples of five

1	2	3	4	5	6	7	8	9	10
11	12	13	14	15	16	17	18	19	20
21	22	23	24	25	26	27	28	29	30
31	32	33	34	35	36	37	38	39	40
41	42	43	44	45	46	47	48	49	50
51	52	53	54	55	56	57	58	59	60
61	62	63	64	65	66	67	68	69	70
71	72	73	74	75	76	77	78	79	80
81	82	83	84	85	86	87	88	89	90
91	92	93	94	95	96	97	98	99	100

Make a pattern by colouring all the numbers
which are multiples of 5.

Solve the puzzle picture opposite by colouring
just those numbers which divide by 5.
What can you see?

Picture Puzzle

six

Six times table

1	X	6	=	
2	X	6	=	
3	X	6	=	
4	X	6	=	
5	X	6	=	
6	X	6	=	
7	X	6	=	
8	X	6	=	
9	X	6	=	
10	X	6	=	
11	X	6	=	
12	X	6	=	

Complete this table.

Multiples of six

1	2	3	4	5	6	7	8	9	10
11	12	13	14	15	16	17	18	19	20
21	22	23	24	25	26	27	28	29	30
31	32	33	34	35	36	37	38	39	40
41	42	43	44	45	46	47	48	49	50
51	52	53	54	55	56	57	58	59	60
61	62	63	64	65	66	67	68	69	70
71	72	73	74	75	76	77	78	79	80
81	82	83	84	85	86	87	88	89	90
91	92	93	94	95	96	97	98	99	100

Make a pattern by colouring all the numbers
which are multiples of 6.

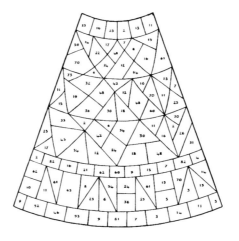

Solve the puzzle picture opposite by colouring
just those numbers which divide by 6.
What can you see?

Picture Puzzle

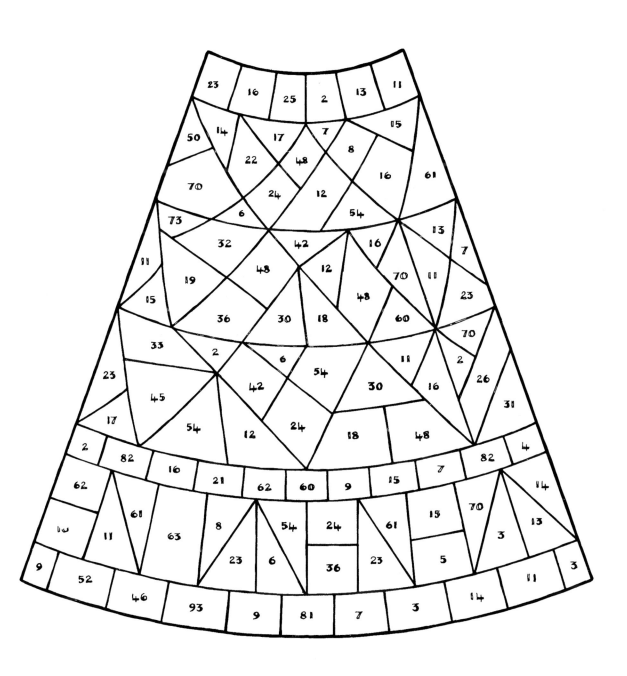

seven

Seven times table

```
 1 X 7 =
 2 X 7 =
 3 X 7 =
 4 X 7 =
 5 X 7 =
 6 X 7 =
 7 X 7 =
 8 X 7 =
 9 X 7 =
10 X 7 =
11 X 7 =
12 X 7 =
```

Complete this table.

Multiples of seven

1	2	3	4	5	6	7	8	9	10
11	12	13	14	15	16	17	18	19	20
21	22	23	24	25	26	27	28	29	30
31	32	33	34	35	36	37	38	39	40
41	42	43	44	45	46	47	48	49	50
51	52	53	54	55	56	57	58	59	60
61	62	63	64	65	66	67	68	69	70
71	72	73	74	75	76	77	78	79	80
81	82	83	84	85	86	87	88	89	90
91	92	93	94	95	96	97	98	99	100

Make a pattern by colouring all the numbers which are multiples of 7.

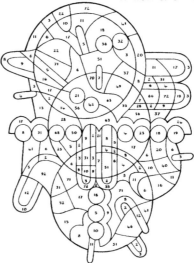

Solve the puzzle picture opposite by colouring just those numbers which divide by 7.
What can you see?

Picture Puzzle

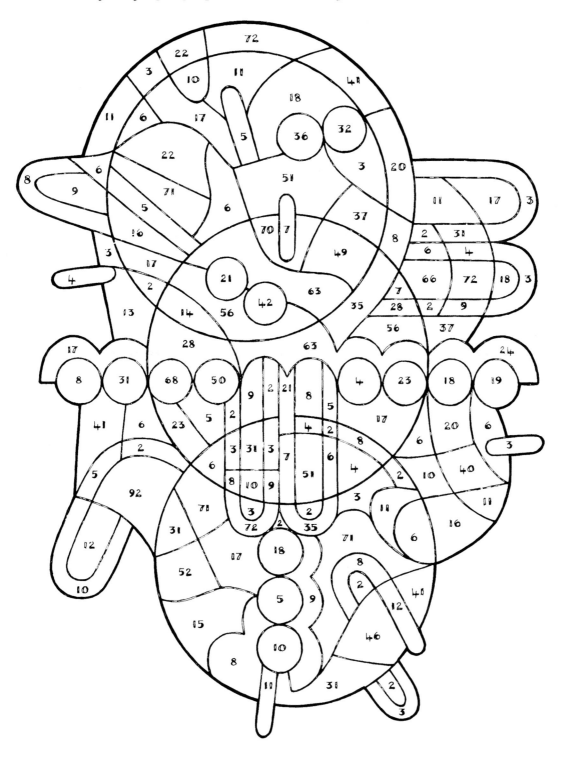

eight

Eight times table

1	×	8	=	
2	×	8	=	
3	×	8	=	
4	×	8	=	
5	×	8	=	
6	×	8	=	
7	×	8	=	
8	×	8	=	
9	×	8	=	
10	×	8	=	
11	×	8	=	
12	×	8	=	

Complete this table.

Multiples of eight

1	2	3	4	5	6	7	8	9	10
11	12	13	14	15	16	17	18	19	20
21	22	23	24	25	26	27	28	29	30
31	32	33	34	35	36	37	38	39	40
41	42	43	44	45	46	47	48	49	50
51	52	53	54	55	56	57	58	59	60
61	62	63	64	65	66	67	68	69	70
71	72	73	74	75	76	77	78	79	80
81	82	83	84	85	86	87	88	89	90
91	92	93	94	95	96	97	98	99	100

Make a pattern by colouring all the numbers
which are multiples of 8.

Solve the puzzle picture opposite by colouring
just those numbers which divide by 8.
What can you see?

8x table

Picture Puzzle

nine

Nine times table

1 X 9 =

2 X 9 =

3 X 9 =

4 X 9 =

5 X 9 =

6 X 9 =

7 X 9 =

8 X 9 =

9 X 9 =

10 X 9 =

11 X 9 =

12 X 9 =

Complete this table.

Multiples of nine

1	2	3	4	5	6	7	8	9	10
11	12	13	14	15	16	17	18	19	20
21	22	23	24	25	26	27	28	29	30
31	32	33	34	35	36	37	38	39	40
41	42	43	44	45	46	47	48	49	50
51	52	53	54	55	56	57	58	59	60
61	62	63	64	65	66	67	68	69	70
71	72	73	74	75	76	77	78	79	80
81	82	83	84	85	86	87	88	89	90
91	92	93	94	95	96	97	98	99	100

Make a pattern by colouring all the numbers
which are multiples of 9.

Solve the puzzle picture opposite by colouring
just those numbers which divide by 9.
What can you see?

9x table

Picture Puzzle

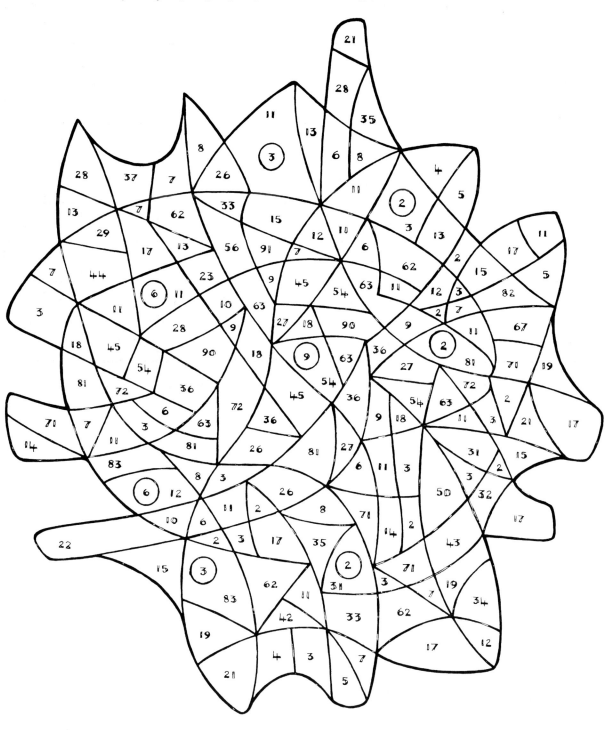

ten

Ten times table

1	X	10	=
2	X	10	=
3	X	10	=
4	X	10	=
5	X	10	=
6	X	10	=
7	X	10	=
8	X	10	=
9	X	10	=
10	X	10	=
11	X	10	=
12	X	10	=

Complete this table.

Multiples of ten

1	2	3	4	5	6	7	8	9	10
11	12	13	14	15	16	17	18	19	20
21	22	23	24	25	26	27	28	29	30
31	32	33	34	35	36	37	38	39	40
41	42	43	44	45	46	47	48	49	50
51	52	53	54	55	56	57	58	59	60
61	62	63	64	65	66	67	68	69	70
71	72	73	74	75	76	77	78	79	80
81	82	83	84	85	86	87	88	89	90
91	92	93	94	95	96	97	98	99	100

Make a pattern by colouring all the numbers
which are multiples of 10.

Solve the puzzle picture opposite by colouring
just those numbers which divide by 10.
What can you see?

Picture Puzzle

eleven

Eleven times table

1	X	11	=	
2	X	11	=	
3	X	11	=	
4	X	11	=	
5	X	11	=	
6	X	11	=	
7	X	11	=	
8	X	11	=	
9	X	11	=	
10	X	11	=	
11	X	11	=	
12	X	11	=	

Complete this table.

Multiples of eleven

1	2	3	4	5	6	7	8	9	10
11	12	13	14	15	16	17	18	19	20
21	22	23	24	25	26	27	28	29	30
31	32	33	34	35	36	37	38	39	40
41	42	43	44	45	46	47	48	49	50
51	52	53	54	55	56	57	58	59	60
61	62	63	64	65	66	67	68	69	70
71	72	73	74	75	76	77	78	79	80
81	82	83	84	85	86	87	88	89	90
91	92	93	94	95	96	97	98	99	100

Make a pattern by colouring all the numbers
which are multiples of 11.

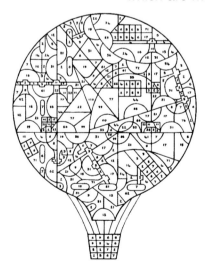

Solve the puzzle picture opposite by colouring
just those numbers which divide by 11.
What can you see?

Picture Puzzle

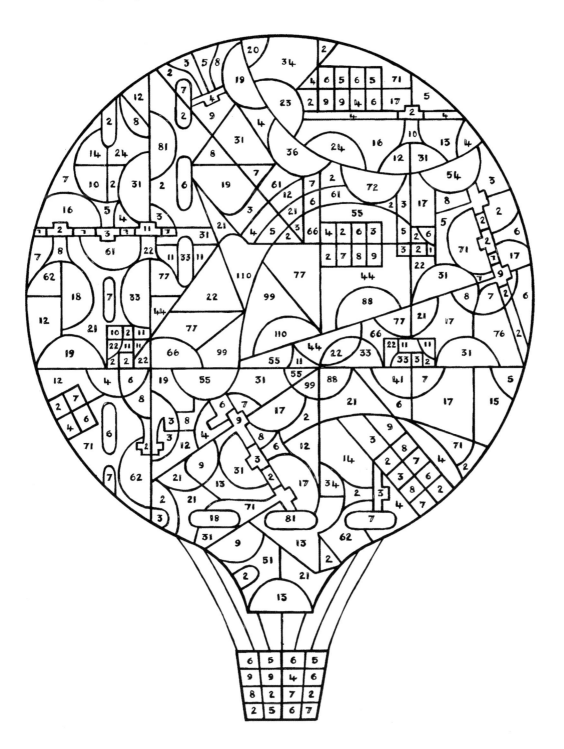

twelve

Twelve times table

1 × 12 =		
2 × 12 =		
3 × 12 =		
4 × 12 =		
5 × 12 =		
6 × 12 =		
7 × 12 =		
8 × 12 =		
9 × 12 =		
10 × 12 =		
11 × 12 =		
12 × 12 =		

Complete this table.

Multiples of twelve

1	2	3	4	5	6	7	8	9	10
11	12	13	14	15	16	17	18	19	20
21	22	23	24	25	26	27	28	29	30
31	32	33	34	35	36	37	38	39	40
41	42	43	44	45	46	47	48	49	50
51	52	53	54	55	56	57	58	59	60
61	62	63	64	65	66	67	68	69	70
71	72	73	74	75	76	77	78	79	80
81	82	83	84	85	86	87	88	89	90
91	92	93	94	95	96	97	98	99	100

Make a pattern by colouring all the numbers
which are multiples of 12.

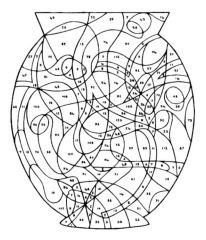

Solve the puzzle picture opposite by colouring
just those numbers which divide by 12.
What can you see?

Picture Puzzle

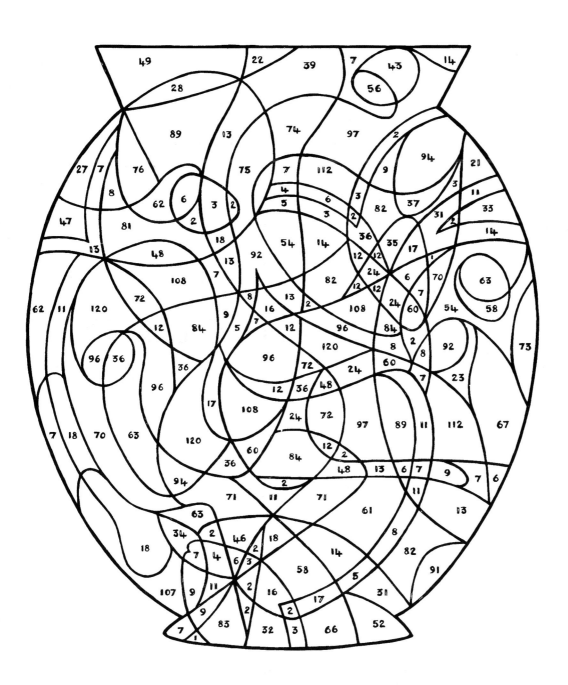

three and five

Three times table

1 X 3 =

2 X 3 =

3 X 3 =

4 X 3 =

5 X 3 =

6 X 3 =

7 X 3 =

8 X 3 =

9 X 3 =

10 X 3 =

11 X 3 =

12 X 3 =

Five times table

1 X 5 =

2 X 5 =

3 X 5 =

4 X 5 =

5 X 5 =

6 X 5 =

7 X 5 =

8 X 5 =

9 X 5 =

10 X 5 =

11 X 5 =

12 X 5 =

You can complete these tables if you wish to.

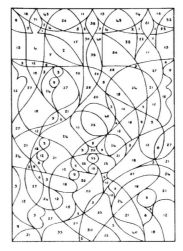

Solve the puzzle picture opposite by colouring
all the numbers which divide by 5 in yellow.
Then colour all the numbers which divide by 3
in a dark colour.
What can you see?

3x and 5x

Double Picture Puzzle

four and seven

		Four times table		
1	X	4	=	
2	X	4	=	
3	X	4	=	
4	X	4	=	
5	X	4	=	
6	X	4	=	
7	X	4	=	
8	X	4	=	
9	X	4	=	
10	X	4	=	
11	X	4	=	
12	X	4	=	

		Seven times table		
1	X	7	=	
2	X	7	=	
3	X	7	=	
4	X	7	=	
5	X	7	=	
6	X	7	=	
7	X	7	=	
8	X	7	=	
9	X	7	=	
10	X	7	=	
11	X	7	=	
12	X	7	=	

You can complete these tables if you wish to.

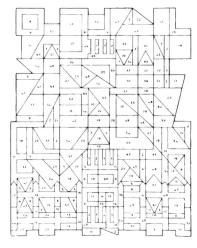

Solve the puzzle picture opposite by colouring
all the numbers which divide by 4 in green.
Then colour all the numbers which divide by 7
in brown.
What can you see?

4x and 7x

Double Picture Puzzle

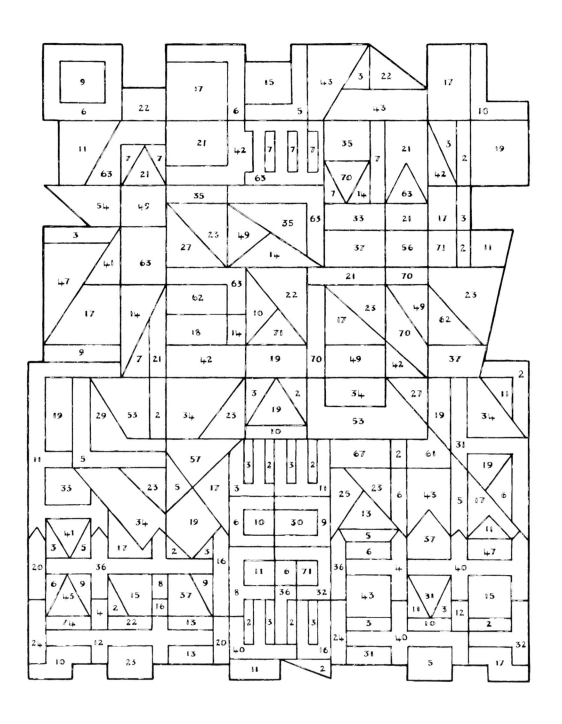

eight and nine

Eight times table	Nine times table

1 X 8 =	1 X 9 =
2 X 8 =	2 X 9 =
3 X 8 =	3 X 9 =
4 X 8 =	4 X 9 =
5 X 8 =	5 X 9 =
6 X 8 =	6 X 9 =
7 X 8 =	7 X 9 =
8 X 8 =	8 X 9 =
9 X 8 =	9 X 9 =
10 X 8 =	10 X 9 =
11 X 8 =	11 X 9 =
12 X 8 =	12 X 9 =

You can complete these tables if you wish to.

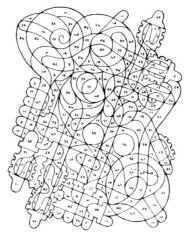

Solve the puzzle picture opposite by colouring
all the numbers which divide by 8 in one colour.
Then colour all the numbers which divide by 9
in another colour.
What can you see?

Double Picture Puzzle

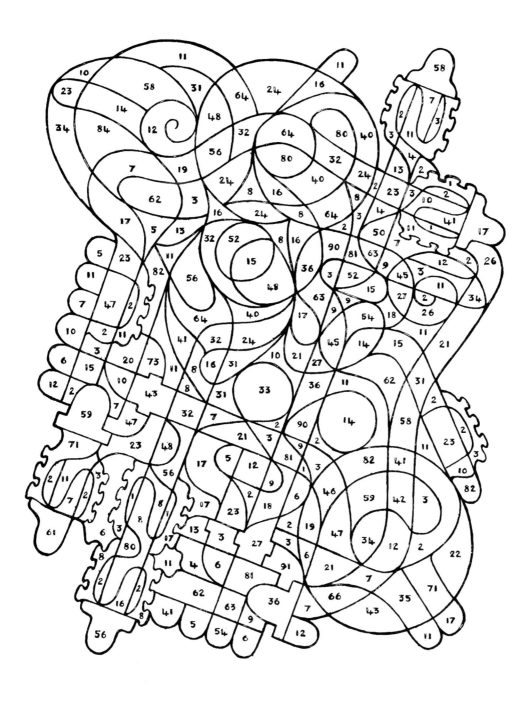

six, ten and eleven

Six times table	Ten times table	Eleven times table
1 X 6 =	1 X 10 =	1 X 11 =
2 X 6 =	2 X 10 =	2 X 11 =
3 X 6 =	3 X 10 =	3 X 11 =
4 X 6 =	4 X 10 =	4 X 11 =
5 X 6 =	5 X 10 =	5 X 11 =
6 X 6 =	6 X 10 =	6 X 11 =
7 X 6 =	7 X 10 =	7 X 11 =
8 X 6 =	8 X 10 =	8 X 11 =
9 X 6 =	9 X 10 =	9 X 11 =
10 X 6 =	10 X 10 =	10 X 11 =
11 X 6 =	11 X 10 =	11 X 11 =
12 X 6 =	12 X 10 =	12 X 11 =

You can complete these tables if you wish to.

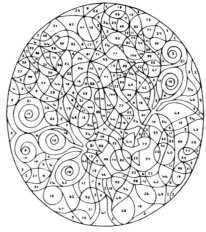

Solve the puzzle picture opposite by colouring
all the numbers which divide by 6 in green.
Then colour those which divide by 11 in red
and those which divide by 10 in yellow.
What can you see?

6x, 10x and 11x

Triple Picture Puzzle

prime numbers

1	2	3	4	5	6	7	8	9	10
11	12	13	14	15	16	17	18	19	20
21	22	23	24	25	26	27	28	29	30
31	32	33	34	35	36	37	38	39	40
41	42	43	44	45	46	47	48	49	50
51	52	53	54	55	56	57	58	59	60
61	62	63	64	65	66	67	68	69	70
71	72	73	74	75	76	77	78	79	80
81	82	83	84	85	86	87	88	89	90
91	92	93	94	95	96	97	98	99	100

This pattern is different from all the others in this book
because it shows all the numbers
which only divide by themselves and 1.
They do not divide by any other number.
Such numbers are called prime numbers.

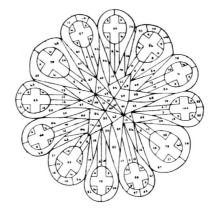

Solve the puzzle picture opposite by colouring
all the prime numbers.
What can you see?